Rein

The **Fiona Harrold** Coaching Series

Reinvent

Your Career

Sue Clarke

7 Steps to the job you love

First published in Great Britain in 2005 by Hodder and Stoughton
A division of Hodder Headline

A Mobius Book

10 9 8 7 6 5 4 3 2 1

A CIP catalogue record for this title is
available from the British Library

ISBN 0 340 83703 9

Typeset in Stone Serif by Palimpsest Book Production Limited,
Polmont, Stirlingshire
Printed and bound by Clays Ltd, St Ives plc

Hodder Headline's policy is to use papers that are natural,
renewable and recyclable products and made from wood grown in
sustainable forests. The logging and manufacturing processes are expected
to conform to the environmental regulations of the country of origin.

Hodder and Stoughton Ltd
A division of Hodder Headline
338 Euston Road
London NW1 3BH

Contents

Acknowledgements

First and foremost, a joyful thanks to Fiona Harrold for making this book possible. Thank you too to Sheila Crowley at AP Watt and everyone at Hodder and Stoughton, in particular my editor, Helen Coyle, whose encouragement and pithy comments have been invaluable. Thanks to Andy Hurdle for his wit, his superbly timed pick-me-up messages and his *Top Gun* aspirations. Thank you Sari Siltala for your unfailing cheerleading, thank you Maureen Smith-Price, especially for an important coffee shop conversation, and thank you Ruth Crawford for your support and friendship throughout. And finally, thank you to my clients. You have all been terrific. I salute every single one of you.

Foreword by Fiona Harrold

Do you want to make your career *and* your life work? Then, read this book! Sue has written a brilliant, practical guide to show you how to do just that. The days of putting up with a job for the money are over. Our parents' generation may have been willing to put life and their deeper desires on hold until retirement age, but not us! Life is just too short and too long to suspend living it as we really want to.

Sue is eminently qualified to coach you towards creating that perfect career and doing work that you love. As the leading career coach on my coaching team, I have seen her support people in turning their lives around and making existing careers work better, or creating entirely new ones. One of her clients shared his transformation on my website recently. With Sue as his coach, David had built up the courage to leave his exhausting job as a manager with a large DIY company, where he had been for ten years and follow his lifelong passion by setting up a landscape gardening business. He continues to work with Sue to build his business, now has a waiting list for his services and is taking on staff. His only regret is that he didn't enlist Sue's help years earlier!

Use Sue as your personal coach. Everything that she shares with you on these pages works. All her tips, techniques and strategies have worked for her and her clients and they'll work for you. She has tested and used all of these in her own life and career. Sue walks her talk and has reinvented her successful career in HR and Management as a brilliant career as a coach and writer. The beauty of what you'll find on these pages is that while you'll be coached to follow your dreams, you'll also be guided in the most practical, workable way to actually make it happen.

Sue will inspire and motivate you. She will give you her 100% support and you must do the same for yourself. Make the effort and get yourself that perfect career and do work that you love. Don't settle for anything less! And get in touch with us at our website, www.fionaharrold.com and tell us about your progress.

Good Luck!

Fiona Harrold
London, 2005

1

What Do You Want?

You are never given a wish without also being given the power to make it true

RICHARD BACH

'I feel stuck.'

'I feel a mild sense of panic most of the time. It's exhausting.'

'I want to do something I've chosen to do, not just fallen into.'

'I feel stale and want to do something new, but I don't know what.'

'I want to stop feeling that "Monday morning feeling", especially as it's ruining Sunday now.'

'I'm in a rut and need help to be dug out.'

'I want to feel fulfilled, to find more purpose and meaning in what I do.'

'I've always dreamed about running my own business; doing my own thing.'

'I know I can do more than this.'

'I look at the painting by Edvard Munch called *The Scream* and I know how he feels.'

These are just a few of the statements my clients have made to me when we've started working together. Perhaps some of them resonate with you. If so, you've come to the right place. Over the next seven chapters, I'm going to coach you in how to get your career back on track so that you're doing work that you love.

I know how staying in the wrong job can deplete you. How it can relentlessly take away your energy and self-esteem. How it can make you restless, frustrated and short-tempered. Leave it too long and you can feel like you're living a slow death. When you're in the wrong job you can undergo a personality change, and it's seldom for the better.

I know about being in the right job too. The 'click'. The feeling of flow. The confidence that comes from knowing that what you do matches what you want to do. Where you feel light, focused, in control. Where rather than hearing clanging, discordant notes in your head, you hear harmony.

HOW TO USE THIS BOOK

To get the most from this book, read it chapter by

chapter, making notes of the things that are important to you. I suggest that you purchase a notebook specifically to record all your thoughts from now on. At various points I'll be encouraging you to do exercises and record the results, but you can use your notebook for any insights and additional thoughts you have along the way too. In the front of your notebook you may like to record all your positive thoughts about what you do want, and at the back you may like to record any thoughts that come to you about what you don't want. At the end of each chapter, give yourself time to review your notes and take any action before starting the next chapter. This way you'll develop your game plan and the blueprint for your perfect career.

I'm going to be your personal coach. Just as I work with my clients, I'm going to work with you. I'll help you to pull out the important things for you, to ask yourself the right questions and I'll bring you focus. I'll help you sort out the jumble in your mind, pinpoint and concentrate on specifics and agree action points to move you forward. I'll coach you so that you can achieve clarity over what you want and the confidence to have a go. You're reading this book because you want better, because deep inside you know that there is better. This book is about finding it. Together we'll build a practical way forward for you that is exciting and inspiring.

HOW DO YOU WANT TO *FEEL* ABOUT THE WORK YOU DO?

You have a feeling, no matter how vague, of what you would like to achieve from the job you do. How close you get to achieving this feeling is the real measure of your happiness at work. It doesn't matter how perfect your job is in theory; if it doesn't press your emotional buttons in the right way it won't be work you love. I've coached many people who open sessions with words like, 'I know I should be happy – some people would kill for my job – but I'm not.' So let's start by becoming intimately acquainted with how you want to *feel* about the work you do.

> The true measure of your happiness at work is feeling that it's right for you

Find a clean sheet in your notebook and head it, 'What I Want from My Job'. Now write down what you want to feel. Be precise. Be explicit. Let the words flow. Fill the page with descriptions of how you want to feel when you wake up on Monday morning; how you want to feel when you tell others about what you do for a living; how you'll feel about your colleagues and your boss; how you'll feel when a new challenge arrives on your desk, whatever that 'desk' comprises. Become emotionally connected with what it's going to be like living your future career. Maybe it's feeling excited, or purposeful, or involved, or full of energy, or free, or playful: choose the words that are right for you. Now up the ante and imagine a picture of yourself in your work: what do you see? Is there laughter, action, verbal sparring, harmony? Again, choose pictures that are right for you. The more senses you can involve the better: what will you hear? Are there smells? Can you touch, taste? Take your time; allow yourself to wallow in what you're creating. This is your future. It's your springboard for where you're going.

WHAT ABOUT THE PRACTICAL STUFF?

Let's put more substance around these feelings and pictures. Continue your brainstorm:

- What are the things you do now that lift your energy?
- What absorbs you?
- Where do you forget yourself?
- What's fun?

There's no need to restrict it to your work experiences – cast the net as wide as you like. List everything that comes into your head. Include past experiences; examples. Don't short-change yourself. Don't censor yourself. List the little things as well as the big ones.

As I write this, Tanya Streeter is the world champion in the extreme sport of free-diving. With nine world records to her name and the ability to slow her heartbeat down to fifteen beats per minute – equivalent to the heart rate of a dolphin – she accomplishes amazingly deep water dives that crush her lungs to the size of lemons. 'I dive for entirely personal reasons, not for the records,' she says. 'I dive to push my potential as a person, not to beat anyone else.'

What are *your* personal reasons? Perhaps a priority for you is being an expert, to practise and develop a particular skill. Or maybe you need to feel constantly challenged and are driven by the need to win – otherwise you know you'll get bored. Perhaps the most important factor for you is that your work fits in with your total lifestyle, balancing your family and your individuality, allowing you the time and energy to enjoy those closest to you. Or perhaps you need to feel that you are caring for people in some way and making a difference to their world.

Now think about what's important to you around work, too:

- What sort of people do you want to work with, and what sort of people contact would you like?
- What type of culture and environment do you prefer?
- What work structure would suit you best – full time, part time, flexible hours?

- What size of organisation attracts you most?
- What location?
- What sort of product or service or business appeals to you?
- What sort of organisation would you be proud to be part of?

What about this:

- What do you need in your work in order to feel in control?
- What makes you feel out of control?

Keep on going. Think about the way you want to be valued and rewarded for the work you do. Find what stands out most for you and add it to your list.

- How much do you want to earn?
- What about benefits and holidays?
- How do you want your pats on the back to be shown?
- What about personal development?

Now over to you: are there any questions you'd like to ask yourself here? Anything we've missed that's important to you? Add the questions and answers to your list. Like a jigsaw puzzle, start by getting all the pieces out of the box. We'll tidy it up and shape it later.

WHAT DO YOU LOVE TO DO?

We often find ourselves doing work that we *can* do rather than work that we actually *enjoy*. It's sometimes easier and seemingly safer to do work simply because we have the ability to do it. It can happen insidiously, too, creeping up on us in apparently innocuous ways, so that over a number of years our careers have taken us to a place that we hardly recognise and where we don't want to be.

Take Carol, who had the 'misfortune' to be a good all-rounder. In a team-building exercise, her skills profile revealed that she'd be good at procedures, a strength lacking in everyone else. Her boss took the deceptively reasonable step of assigning procedural matters to her, and these tasks came to occupy more and more of her time and objectives. The fact that Carol didn't enjoy this sort of work was overlooked, and Carol herself underestimated the impact that agreeing to take the work on would have on her general motivation. It wasn't long before she began to lose her usual enthusiasm and energy. She became literally bogged down in processes and paperwork, whereas what she enjoyed was being actively out there on the front line making things happen. There's always a double whammy when something like this happens. For Carol, a feeling of disempowerment subtly encroached; she started to lose confidence in herself and the longer it went on the more she began to forget what it was she enjoyed doing in the first place.

Make sure you start from a place where you suspend any thinking about what you *can* do (we'll come to that in chapter 3). Focus on what you enjoy doing. Include your interests, your hobbies. Go right back to when you were a child too. Get out of your head and into your body and listen to yourself. Look back over everything you've done in the past and single out the times when your energy was high and you felt light. Compare those with times when your energy dragged and you felt heavy. Add the triggers for feeling light to your list of Job Wants. My guess is that these are the things you find intrinsically rewarding; things you'd do even if you didn't have to.

> High energy and lightness are clear signals to find work you love

HOW CAN YOU BE TRUE TO YOU?

I'd like to know what you value. When you live in accordance with your values, you have a sense of being true to yourself and you're at your best, body and soul. You feel genuine, natural and authentic. The same applies to work. To be true to ourselves in our work we need to connect with our values and make sure that what we value has expression in the work that we do. If you're changing yourself to fit in with your company's ethics and values, it won't be your perfect work. Let's check out *your* values.

- What's most important to you in your life?
- What and who inspire you?
- What won't you compromise?
- How would you summarise your best qualities?
- What do you like and admire most about your friends?
- What qualities have your best bosses and teachers had?
- What organisations do you admire most and why?
- What makes you proud?

If any material objects appear on your 'important' list, look for the meaning behind the object. Ask yourself what makes that object important to you, what does it give you? You may say your car is important to you. If I ask you what your car means to you, perhaps you'll say you like the sense of freedom and excitement it gives you to drive fast, or maybe it's the status and prestige you feel; the reliability and security; or maybe it's simply the feeling of fun that erupts when you see and drive that car.

Let's consider some of the values people have

described to me over the years. Autonomy, for instance: a dislike of rules and preferring to be left to do things your own way, at your own pace and to your own standards. Security: a desire for the future to be reasonably predictable and stable. Creativity: wanting to express your imagination and resourcefulness in your work. Or how about freedom, choice, balance, simplicity, spontaneity, learning and intellectual curiosity, responsibility, honesty, quality?

Take time to determine your values. There are no right or wrong answers. The only condition is that the values you choose are ones that have most meaning and importance to *you*. If you catch yourself choosing a value that you think you should have, stop and ask yourself whether this is truly your value, or is, in fact, someone else's idea of what's important. If you hear a 'should' or an 'ought' in your head, ask yourself simply, 'according to whom?' Go through your list of values and check there aren't any impostors. If you find any, take them out. Now rank your values in order. Which values are most important to you? What are your priorities?

What does this tell you about you? If I were to ask you to describe what was most important to you in your life and your work, how would you answer? What does it tell you about the sort of work you'll love? What does it tell you about the sort of work you *won't*? Consider the mismatch, for instance, if you're working in a highly competitive environment, where the focus is on individual effort and results, and your priority values are co-operation and teamwork.

> When you understand your values, you have vital clues about the type of work you'll love

I regularly hear clients acknowledge that they've ended up where they are because they've done what they thought they were supposed to do, what other people thought best, what was 'sensible' or 'logical' or because everyone else was doing it. Take Sandy, who had landed an interview with a prestigious European institution. Her friends and parents were pushing her to go for it, but her heart just wasn't in it. She found it difficult to come right out and say so though, because the arguments her family and friends used were so 'right'. So we took a sheet of paper and split it into two columns, heading one: 'What other people say', and the other: 'What's important to me'. This is what we found:

What other people say

- It's a prestigious company
- It'll look great on your CV
- The job's secure
- It's fantastic money

- Think of the credibility you'll gain
- What have you got to lose from just going for the interview?

What's important to me

- I want to go freelance
- I want to be responsible for myself
- I want to choose my own projects
- I don't want to work for a bureaucratic institution again
- I don't want to go to an interview and waste people's time
- I don't want to set myself up for interview rejection

Next, we went down the list of 'what other people say' and asked: Is this important to me, and if so, on a scale of one to ten, how important? Needless to say, the result was that what other people valued, Sandy didn't. Once she was able to tune in to her own values, it made everything so much easier. Her energy was no longer consumed fighting the tension between 'should do' and 'want to do' and, able to align with her true needs, she could move forward in the direction she wanted to go.

Back to you. Are you clear about what's important to you, what *you* value most highly? Then make sure you've noted it all down.

THE WORK

1. Where are you starting from? If I asked you how you felt before you started to read this book, what would you answer? Would you pick any of the statements I've listed at the beginning, or would it be something else? Write it down at the back of your notebook. This is where we want to move you from.

2. Where would you like to end up? Where is it you want to move to? What would be the opposite of what you've just put in the back of your notebook, for instance? Ensure you've used positive not negative words. What sort of timescale would you like to put on achieving that? Write it all down, this time at the very front, as the very first thing you have in your notebook. This is your objective.

3. How do you want to feel about the work that you do? Imagine watching a movie of yourself, one of those where a voiceover comes in and explains how you're feeling; what would that voiceover say? Start it like this: 'This is me, at work, just a normal day, and I feel . . .'

4. Connect with your values. Discover what's meaningful to you, and just as importantly, what's meaning*less*. This is about you and nobody else; what you want in your life and what you don't. Consider what place you're giving your values in your life and work today. Which ones are you compromising? What are you going to do about that? Start right now.

5. Create your list of job wants. Get practical, get explicit. Think it through. Feel it – get out of your head for a while and into your body. Where is your energy high and light? Get in touch with what fires you up, where you feel most alive. Get clear about the essence of what it is you want.

Key idea

Start from a basis of what you enjoy; the rest will follow naturally.

2

Find the Real You

Life is a sum of all your choices

ALBERT CAMUS

In chapter 1 we concentrated on clarifying what you want from your work. Now I'd like us to dig a little deeper, to uncover what might not be immediately apparent: to look beneath the surface and make sure that we tease out what's less obvious, but just as – if not even more – important to you.

SEE THE BIGGER PICTURE

Let me ask you this question: How's your *life* right now? Often when I first talk to clients, the person starts from the certainty that their job is 'the problem'. When I spend a little time with them looking at the bigger picture of their life, though, many find that their view of their job has become distorted. They feel dissatisfied with their lot, yes, but sometimes it's easier to blame work rather than confront the fact that their whole life needs a bit of an overhaul.

Work can be a symptom. The danger with diving off into fixing your career is that often this can blur the picture of what really needs to be fixed. The reality is that focusing on your career in isolation is often not the best way forward and sometimes downright counter-productive. So, before we start on your career, let's spend a little time on how your life is right now.

Focus on things like social life, fun, hobbies, how you express yourself creatively, friends, family, health, romance, your spiritual life, how you contribute to society, the physical environment you live in, how much personal growth you're banking. Create a checklist of these key things. Add other factors that are important to you. If I asked you to score your satisfaction in each of the items on your list on a scale of one to ten, how would you do? Are you the person you expected to be at this stage of your life? If you're not as content as you could be in any area, if you find some gaps between how you want your life to be and what you've got, start filling in those gaps. Be sure that you're not using your career as a scapegoat, as an excuse to avoid the issues in the larger pattern of your life.

Home in on the real problem; tackle it at source. Sadly, people continue to arrive on my doorstep burnt out and dissatisfied because they've devoted their lives to their careers and neglected the wider perspective. Some are driven to perform and be successful and as a result repress their need for close and nurturing relationships. If this is where you're headed, take stock now. Make sure there's time and space for all the things on your checklist – and there's no need to wait until you feel happier in your work. You'll find that the one positively impacts on the other.

> Make sure your career is part of your life, not its entirety

Let me tell you about Sara. Sara came to see me because she was dissatisfied in her job as a partner in an international law firm. She was successful and well respected. She earned an excellent salary that funded a number of exciting hobbies, which she greatly enjoyed. 'On paper' things looked great. But Sara was unhappy and felt strongly that her job was the problem. She didn't know what she wanted to change to, and she knew that her lifestyle was important and any alternative career options would have to support her financial needs. But what was also lacking in Sara's life was close personal relationships – at any level. When we first started talking, she was convinced that working in the legal field had encouraged this; she felt she had become cold, judgemental and disconnected. Staying in the law, she believed, would just make matters worse. Hence her decision to change.

With her real needs in mind, we agreed an agenda specifically to release her warm and friendly personality. She started with simple steps: at work, making opportunities to spend time with her team, her colleagues, her superiors, rather than rushing past them to 'get the job done'. Her remit was to get to know them as people and allow them to get to know her as a person too. In her personal life, Sara started to renew her contacts with acquaintances she'd long lost touch with, and to take every opportunity to be friendly to new people she met.

Sara had to overcome some considerable fears in opening up in this way. On one level, fear of feeling stupid, having her overtures ignored, rejected – after all, she'd been someone very different for quite a while now. On another level, fear of losing the respect of her colleagues and bosses, who saw her as highly efficient and focused. Allowing her true needs to be expressed meant stepping outside her comfort zone which wasn't easy or without risk.

Once she started to express a vital part of who she was, though – a warm, friendly, open person who needed to connect with the people around her – a subtle transformation started to take place. Her social life began to blossom. She found her colleagues and bosses responded positively; her fears of rejection had been groundless. Her job started to feel better, she began to see it in a new and positive light. Sara is still a lawyer, and happy now to continue to be so. Concentrating her energy on her job was the wrong road; the right one was to focus on what she was making of her life.

CREATE A TIME LINE

I'd like you to imagine yourself at eighty years old, looking back on your life. What do you need to accomplish during your lifetime for you to consider your life to have been fulfilling and well lived? Come back to the present day. Are you creating what you need for a happy life on your terms? What lifestyle do you need for those accomplishments to happen, and are you building it?

Fill in the detail a little more by imagining a time line from now forwards. If you want a family, for instance, where will that fit in, and what impact will it have? What about travel and adventures – big mountains you want to climb? long journeys you want to make? oceans you want to sail? – where will those fit in? How about courses you want to take? What about the other, significant, people in your life: where do their needs sit on your time line? As you build your time line, you build perspective and start to gain an appreciation of how and where your career fits into your life. It makes you think more deeply about what you really want out of life and how you can achieve it.

Rachel was very clear that she wanted to achieve a 'big push forward' at work. She enjoyed her job, but felt that her skills and talents weren't being fully used and she knew she could do the job of the grade above her, perhaps even better than those doing it already. She felt that if she didn't go for it, she'd regret it, that she'd be letting herself down. Reflecting on the eighty-year-old question, a wider perspective emerged, though. She was thirty-three and happily married, and was thinking about starting a family. Having a family was definitely on her list of life accomplishments. Mulling over how the promotion would change her lifestyle, she began to realise that it would conflict with her idea of being a good parent. Rachel then admitted that although she had set herself an objective of promotion, she also felt a tension inside; she felt confused, so much so that sometimes she felt like running away. She'd put these feelings down to lack of self-confidence, doubt as to whether she could cut it at a higher level job-wise. By building her time line, she realised this wasn't the case at all; her feelings of discomfort were about whether this promotion would really give her what she wanted.

Build your time line to build perspective about how your career fits into your life

LISTEN TO YOUR INTUITION

The key to helping Rachel identify what she really wanted was a feeling of conflict inside. Maybe you have similar feelings? Or maybe your conflicts show themselves in more physical ways – through migraines, or frequent colds, or insomnia, or muscular aches, or stomach ache, for instance. However they reveal themselves, if you have feelings of conflict I recommend that you don't ignore them. Rather, listen up; tune in. Often discomfort is a clear signal to us from our intuition and if we pay attention to it, it can clarify what we want to do. Feelings of anxiety and pain can be a meaningful and powerful communication about being our true selves.

Discomfort can be good: it tells us what we need to do if only we stay long enough to listen

Intuition can also show itself in more positive ways. As you're pondering what you want to do, notice any gut feelings you have, any ideas or images that pop into your head, no matter how unrealistic or ridiculous they may seem at first. The same goes for feelings of longing, which can be deep signals from our subconscious about where we need to be heading. Don't suppress these feelings or thoughts. Focus on them, tease them out: what do they really mean? What clues are they giving you about the work you will love to do?

Emma was popular and fun-loving; she enjoyed her life; it was full and active. She'd held many jobs in her working life. She'd worked successfully in PR, she'd been an estate agent and earned top commission, a charity events organiser, arranging people from all over the world in acts of philanthropy, a reflexologist, she'd temped – but whatever she did she continued to feel a sense of rootlessness and restlessness that affected her ability to settle in her work. Emma also experienced feelings of longing to move to Spain. She'd started by bottling up this longing, considering it silly and unrealistic, a hare-brained fantasy stimulated by watching too many programmes on places in the sun. Gradually though, as the longing continued, she allowed herself truly to listen to herself. She borrowed Spanish language tapes from the local library and started to teach herself Spanish. She viewed Spanish property websites, just to see what they contained. A little while later she bumped into an old colleague of hers who told her he was setting up an estate agency to deal with Spanish properties. He asked her whether she would be interested in working with him again, running the Spanish office. Was it a coincidence? Probably. But I suggest that if you listen to your longing it will increase your odds of serendipitous discovery. Maybe it will be the air pocket in your upturned boat. Open your mind to the benefit of intuitive leaps. If you have a hunch, give it road room. See where it takes you. Add your hunches to your list of Job Wants.

FIND YOUR SENSE OF PURPOSE

Psychological studies consistently report that we're happiest when we do something we believe makes a difference. We're happiest in a job we find worthwhile. In fact, we often work harder for fewer rewards when what we do links to our deepest beliefs. Is this what you need? Connect now with what would make your work meaningful and contributory, what would give you a sense of innermost achievement. If you were to create a mission statement for yourself, what would it be?

Make sure it answers these questions:

- What do you feel passionate about?
- What makes you angry?
- What do you want to be involved with?
- What do you want to change?
- How do you want to make your mark?

Consider Monty Roberts, the man who developed the method for communicating with horses called 'horse whispering'. He was spurred on by a deep sense of injustice at the way some people ill-treat horses and his fervent belief that violence has no place in our relationship with them. He knew what he felt passionate about, he knew what he felt angry about, what he wanted to change. He went on to make his mark as the man who ensured that today we all know about the kind alternative to managing fractious or nervous horses.

When Estée Lauder died last year, newspapers the world over saluted her pioneering spirit, and drew attention to how her quest for self-improvement fuelled her business acumen so that she became one of the most prominent women in the worlds of both commerce and society. Her career started at high school when she brought her school friends home to try out the face creams her chemist uncle made. From these humble beginnings, she developed a beauty business that made her a cosmetics tycoon, and a household icon to millions of women. She called her wares 'jars of hope' and told women they could 'start the new year with a new face'. A fervent believer in her own products, she travelled continually to ensure her sales force lived up to her example.

The common factor in these two very different stories is that both people felt that they were improving the world in some way. If you were to feel that you were improving your world, what would that mean in your terms? It doesn't have to be something huge, or grand, you can 'think global, act local' as the slogan goes.

> Home in on what will make you feel rich inside

Maybe, as was the case for a good friend of mine, it means shifting the emphasis of the work you do; in his case, turning down a lucrative international job offer because it would have meant devoting his considerable skills to a business that gave him no sense of personal enrichment. We're all different. The trick is to home in on what would make *you* feel rich inside. Where would you be if you wore your convictions on your sleeve? Add your thoughts to your list of Job Wants.

CAN YOU HEAR YOU?

If you're still struggling to define what you want, listen to what's going on in your head. Do you hear lots of noise, disjointed conversations, like a radio that's out of tune? Or is there a huge vacuum, an unfathomable black hole of silence? Are you paralysed by all the thinking you're doing? Just going round in circles and not getting anywhere? Sitting on the fence because no side seems greener? Maybe you're so used to pleasing others that you simply can't connect with what will please *you*? Do you have your own space, or is everyone else in it?

Until you can create space for yourself, you won't have room to hear what you want, no matter how hard you listen. So if this is you, step back. Take some time out. Read again about being true to you in chapter 1; reconnect with what's important to you, rather than what's important to everyone else. Focus on the bigger picture of your life, and take action to build a life that's full and balanced. Gradually you'll find that you start to hear the sound of your own voice. And it will be sweet. Do what Michelangelo did: see your angel in the marble and carve until you set it free.

THE WORK

1. See your career in its true perspective. How's your *life* right now? Check that your job is the whole issue. Sometimes it's easier for us to blame our jobs when the truth is that our lives need an overhaul. If you need to reshape your life, don't procrastinate, hoping that changing your job will miraculously change your life. It will make a difference, but it can't compensate for a lack of close and nurturing relationships, good health, social pleasure, personal growth.

2. Construct your time line. What do you want to accomplish in your life? What will make your life feel well lived when you're eighty years old? How does the work you do fit with this?

3. Listen to your intuition, even if it's uncomfortable. Discomfort can be good: it can tell you what you need to do if only you stay long enough to listen.

4. Identify what gives you a sense of purpose. We're happiest when we feel that we are making a difference to our world. What would be a worthwhile and motivating mission for you? How could you express that in the work you do?

5. Make sure you can hear *you*. Create the space you need so that you can tune in to what you're telling yourself.

Key idea

Find the real you, and when you've found it, follow it.

3

What Are You Good At?

The truth is that all of us attain the greatest success and happiness possible in this life whenever we use our capacities to their greatest extent

ANONYMOUS

Every day you're gaining experience. Skills. Knowledge. Sometimes what you're gaining is tangible, you're aware of the shift. At other times the process is so gradual that it's only when you look back to a specific moment that you're able to appreciate how far you've come. Sometimes it's so subtle that you don't even realise it's happened.

Each time we move jobs we use many of the abilities we've already developed. Every job prepares us in some way for the next one. It may not be immediately apparent, but the skills you've learned and the knowledge and experience you've gained will be of value to you in your perfect work. Whatever you are doing now is helping you to gain skills, experience, knowledge, or ways of thinking and being that will be useful in the future. Nothing is wasted. Everything has importance and relevance.

What we're going to focus on now is this: among the experience you've gained, the knowledge and the skills, what is it that you do well? Where is it that you consistently deliver? What can you be relied on to get right? Where are you the person that everyone wants to have around? You'll need to start a fresh section in your notebook for this. Record your thoughts diligently, as we'll be using them later.

WHAT KNOWLEDGE AND SKILLS DO YOU HAVE?

We pick up knowledge and skills from diverse sources. Your formal education and qualifications are important, and rightly belong on your list, just as the knowledge you've gained through your jobs does. Think these through now and make sure your notebook summarises the experience and knowledge and skills you have gained.

Think more broadly as well. How much have you developed knowledge and skills from the conversations you've had, the books you've read, the journeys you've made, the workshops and courses you've attended, any voluntary or community or social activities you've participated in? List whatever you've accumulated. Are your skills with people, animals, ideas, facts, figures, practical things? Are you good with detail, or the broader picture? What roles bring out the best in you? What roles do other people think you're good at? What knowledge and skills do you have that have made you the person you are today?

> Take the time to assemble your skills and knowledge portfolio. I guarantee it'll contain more than you expect

WHAT DO YOU DO WELL?

Make a study of the areas where you consistently deliver quality work, situations where you excel. Think about the work you do now, and what you've done in the past. Again, don't forget to think outside your work too. One of my former colleagues could always be relied upon to deliver excellent presentations at our customer meetings. He had a talent for being able to extract what customers needed to know, the self-discipline and calmness under pressure always to make sure he prepared in good time and the confidence to deliver what he had to say in an accessible and relaxed style. Interestingly, his talent for presenting was recognised at work only quite late on in his career, although it emerged that it followed years of expression and refinement through his interest in adventure travel and the talks he gave about his trips, where he regularly presented to dozens of people of all ages and backgrounds.

Bestselling author Joanne Harris writes books that have caught the public's imagination in the way they portray pleasures of the senses. Read the cover of *Chocolat*, for example, and what's striking is the numerous references to how she excels in conveying the sensual pleasures of taste and smell. Critics acclaim her gift for transporting us to Vianne's *chocolaterie*, to lean on the padded counter and sip a cup of *chocolat*. Her talent for words that can fire our senses in this way is impressive, and it's one of her major strengths.

What about you? What are your major strengths? Where do you excel, or do your best work? Where are your highest achievements? What are the things you're most proud of? This is where you make a difference, where you shine. How could you do more of these things? Spend time pondering and record the results in your notebook.

> Identify what you do well and seek out every opportunity to demonstrate it

WHAT DO YOU *NOT* DO WELL?

Just as important as knowing what you do well is understanding what you don't. When you do things well, your self-esteem rises and you feel good about yourself. If you work as part of a team, doing things well can help you feel you're making a valuable contribution, that what you do is worthwhile, that you belong. When you struggle with things, the opposite happens. You rapidly lose confidence in yourself, work loses its meaning and you can become alienated from your colleagues. There's a difference here between things you don't do well but could learn to do well, and things that you don't do well no matter how hard you work at it. I'm talking about the latter.

> Understanding what makes you struggle and steering clear is crucial to finding work you love

When Alan came to see me he'd been made redundant, and anxious and wary eyes looked out at me from behind his glasses. He'd struggled in his job as an IT manager; as a result his confidence was already fragile and the additional blow of redundancy had poleaxed him. He dreaded the thought of having to look for work.

Investigating Alan's situation, it became clear that he had been promoted beyond what he was best at, and that his career over the last three years had been an exercise in getting through each day without anyone noticing he wasn't coping very well. We needed to go back in time three years to when he was excelling as a programmer to begin understanding what it was Alan was good at, to start to reconnect him with his strengths. Once we'd accomplished this, we were able to draw a clear line between what Alan did well – and what he didn't.

Make sure you've drawn your clear line too. What do you do well – and what do you not? What will you look for? And what will you steer clear of? Pop it down in your notebook.

WHAT ABOUT YOUR NATURAL TALENTS?

What are the things that come easily to you? Recognise these and you're well on your way to identifying your natural, innate talents. Our innate talents may show themselves in our work, or they may reveal themselves in the other things we do.

Tim was a successful sales executive who until recently had enjoyed his job. However, his enthusiasm had started to wane. He'd had a spell as a manager, but that hadn't suited him: he didn't enjoy the administrative aspects that came with the job, nor did he relish the sudden loss in satisfaction and credit he got from consistently delivering his personal sales targets.

There was no doubt that Tim was a terrific role model for sales people and that he had excellent selling skills across diverse products and markets. When we explored his natural talents, the things that came easily to him, here is what he listed:

- At ease with anyone; able to talk to anyone
- Humour (he was known for his wit)
- Being organised; neat and tidy
- Independent
- Individual
- Picking up foreign languages (accompanied by a degree in German)
- Teaching (when he'd left university he'd started out as a teacher and had found it came naturally to him, but had left because of the low pay)
- Giving presentations
- Being on stage and in the limelight (he was part of a local amateur dramatics group)

When we looked at how much Tim could use these natural talents in his work, what we found was that the majority of them were untapped. His working environment was very serious and he felt inhibited and unable to express his natural humour. His ability to be independent and individual was constrained by the strict protocols he had to follow. He had no opportunity to use his natural flair for languages or teaching.

He did give presentations but they were usually in the form of serious meetings, often one-to-one, and gave no outlet for his natural showmanship. When he reflected, he acknowledged that it was only his high self-motivation and discipline that had kept him going in what were in fact hostile conditions for doing work he loved.

What about you? Take some time now to think about your natural talents, the things that come easily to you.

> Natural talents are a short cut to finding work you love – they show you the work that loves you

WHAT COULD YOU DEVELOP?

When you're thinking about the things you're good at, don't forget the areas that you could develop. If you have an interest in a particular subject, find ways to pursue that interest and learn more. If there's an area of your work where you have less experience, target it: investigate how you could increase your experience so that you feel confident and able. The profile of what you do well is continually evolving. You can accelerate this natural process by actively seeking out ways to add to your skills and knowledge.

Mandy had begun her career as a nurse, moved to

health visiting and then on to run her own business as an aromatherapist. More and more, she found herself acting as an informal counsellor as well, as she realised that her clients needed healing words as well as healing hands. Although all her working life she had spent time listening to clients' problems, she felt uneasy about the level of counselling she was undertaking. So she enrolled on a psychotherapy course and studied hard while continuing her aromatherapy practice.

When she started out on the course, she had no plans to become a full-time counsellor; her wish was to develop her counselling skills so that she could better meet the needs of her clients. At first she intended to do a one-year basic course, but that turned into a further year, until finally she was doing the full diploma. Over time, more and more clients wanted Mandy for her talking cure, and her counselling caseload started to outweigh her massage one until eventually she became a full-time counsellor and supervisor for other therapists. It wasn't easy: it was tiring and demanding making a four-year commitment to study, with a family and a busy practice, attending a tough lecture schedule with travel to London from the Midlands. But by developing her skills in response to her feeling of need, in a way that seemed right and natural, Mandy built her career in a rewarding way.

What about you? How could you develop your skills and knowledge? Where could you expand, what could you deepen? What options do you have to widen your opportunities right now? What insights could this provide into doing work that you love?

> Be constantly alert to how you can deepen and expand what you already have

WHAT'S YOUR GIFT?

When working with my clients, I've consistently found that each person has a special quality that's present throughout their working life, something that stands out about them and the way they do their work. It's something that's always there when they're doing work at their best. I call it their gift. Conversely, if there's no outlet for expressing their gift, work can feel stale and meaningless and the quality of the work they do can be adversely affected. To illustrate, let me share the stories of three of my recent clients.

Barry had been a mechanical engineer most of his working life and in his late forties was made redundant. His redundancy payout offered the opportunity to buy a business from a former friend who was retiring, and he grasped it with both hands. He was excited by being his own boss and doing his own thing. Within twelve months, however, he was feeling stifled and stagnant.

Plus, his formerly robust self-esteem and confidence were under threat.

When we explored the themes that ran through Barry's working life, one factor stood out above all the rest: Barry was always the one who created the first of anything. He had created new designs and submitted numerous patent applications in his engineering career. His major strength was innovation: finding the solution to an insoluble problem, and then moving on to the next one. When he'd opened for business, Barry had initially relished the challenge of starting something new. But the business was already running pretty smoothly, so there was little opportunity for him to be innovative. The gift that had been with Barry from childhood was unable to be expressed. As a consequence, what had started out as an exciting project rapidly turned into dull, routine work.

Then there's Susie. Susie's gift was helping people. Whatever line of work she was in, and she had been in several, an enduring characteristic was that Susie was good at helping people. Even when she moved on to a new department, her old customers rang her when they had a problem because they had confidence that she would sort things out for them. Susie didn't relish problem-solving for itself, but when a customer had a problem her overriding drive was to help them to solve it.

Finally, Jo. When Jo came to see me, she was feeling highly stressed and overwhelmed by her work. Her job as PA to the managing director in a start-up business contained lots of variety, no two days were the same, and she needed to be able to juggle multiple tasks at one time. When we delved into the themes in Jo's working life we discovered that where she worked best, however, was where there was structure and routine and clear boundaries. The opposite to what she had! Where many of her colleagues abhorred the thought of doing detailed and intricate documents, this was where Jo excelled. It was her gift. Jo is now a highly regarded legal secretary – and loves it.

> Identify what's consistently present when you're doing well. It's another clue to the work you'll love

Are you like Barry, an innovator, relishing the challenge of creating something new? Are you at your best when there's a thorny problem to solve? Are you like Susie, or Jo? Or maybe your gift is something entirely different. Think about it. Take time to ponder the themes in your working life, and what they tell you about the type of work you do best.

WHAT ABOUT YOUR ATTITUDES?

Maybe it sounds strange to discuss 'attitudes' in a

chapter on what you can do. If so, let me explain, because they are crucial. Think about the people you currently work with or you've worked with in the past. What sort of things stand out to you? Yes, you will recall their experience and their knowledge and their talents and their skills; these are all important factors in how well they do their jobs, how much you can rely on them to help you when you need it. But the additional factor is their *attitude*, their approach to their work, to people. It's quite tough to define what we mean when we say it, but we've all said at one point or another: 'She's got the right attitude'; 'His attitude is appalling.' The attitude a person brings to their work makes an immense difference to how good they are at it.

Take something close to my own heart, customer service. When I came back from working in Australia, I was fired up about good customer service. What I had experienced in Australia, especially in the company I worked for, showed me what a great attitude towards customer service was all about – so much so that it inspired me to make one of my biggest career changes! Some time later in my career when I was recruiting and managing my own customer service team, attitude was at the top of the list of things I looked for. Experience, knowledge, skills – these were all important, but if the person didn't have the right attitude it just didn't work. I'm sure I'm not alone here: how many of us have been on the wrong side of a bad attitude and suffered the consequences?

> Your attitude is a huge differentiator in how good you are at what you do. It also sends an eloquent message about work you love, and work you don't

Reflect on your own attitudes, especially the ones where you just know you're good. This is different from skills, from experience, from knowledge, isn't it? Maybe you've got a great attitude to customer service (hurrah!), or maybe you can't stop yourself looking to improve things (complacency just isn't in your vocabulary), or maybe you're the sort of person who can't and won't stand back when you see injustice happening. Go deep on this one, do a bit of soul searching. It's worth it. Record your conclusions in your notebook.

HOW DO OTHER PEOPLE VIEW YOU?

Sometimes, the things we can do, the things we're good at, natural at, our experience, our knowledge, our skills, are so close to us that we don't appreciate them. We take them for granted. We underrate them. Sometimes we can't even see them. At a Fiona Harrold workshop I helped to run last year, one of the participants, when asked what things she was good at, simply couldn't answer. I didn't know this woman, I hadn't seen her before or talked to her, but one thing had struck me as soon as she spoke: her voice. It was soft, sweet, warm, gentle. Yet until then she was totally unaware of this asset.

Why am I telling you this? Because in gathering all your information about what you're good at, make sure you ask other people what they think too. Choose friends and family members and colleagues whom you trust and respect. If it's not covered in your next performance review at work, ask the question. If you don't have a review, ask the question anyway. You may have some pleasant surprises.

THE WORK

1. **Build your skills and knowledge portfolio.** Review your experience, and what it's taught you. Identify where you have your biggest achievements. What skills drive your success? What knowledge underpins your results? How could you develop these things further?

2. **Identify your natural talents.** Recognise the things you do that flow, that come easily to you. Notice the things that others may struggle with that you don't. Become aware of what you contribute simply by being you. How could you express them more?

3. Find your gift. What theme runs through your work? Unravel the thread that knits your working life together. Find what's consistently present when you're doing well.

4. Determine what others seek you out for. Get to know yourself as others do. How do your colleagues, your family, your friends view you? What can they see that you take for granted?

5. Examine your attitudes. What makes you stand out? What makes you distinctive? What's the extra ingredient you bring to any work that you do?

Key idea

Identify everything you do well. Now develop these things so you do them even better.

4

Your Ideal Work

Every man has his own vocation

RALPH WALDO EMERSON

In this chapter, we'll pull together what you've discovered about yourself in chapters 1, 2 and 3. You've done a lot of work, so let's make sure we capture it. We'll summarise what, ideally, you would like to be present in the work you do. We'll compare this with what you have in reality in your work at the moment. We'll identify where the biggest gaps are and what you can do about them to move forward into work you love.

CREATE YOUR CAREER WHEEL

I'd like you to study the diagram below. This is your

Career Wheel and we're going to categorise the notes you've made according to its sections. There are four steps:

1. You'll summarise what you ideally want in your work using each section of the Career Wheel.

2. You'll examine what you have right now in your work to determine where there are matches with your ideal and where there are gaps.

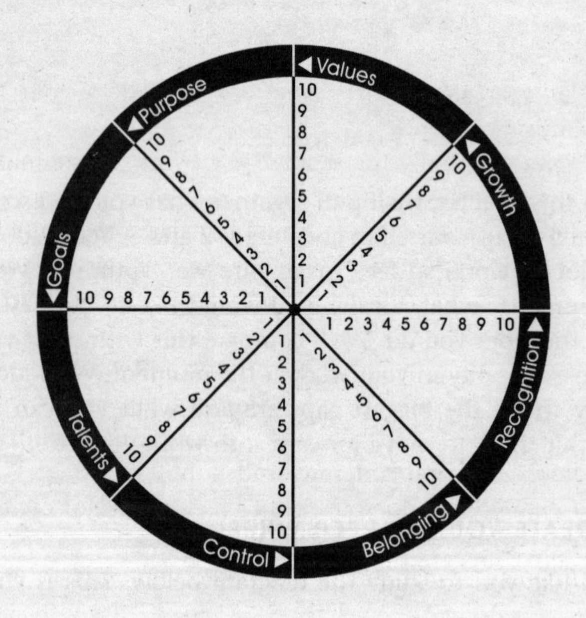

3. You'll allocate a satisfaction rating to each section of your wheel, together with an importance rating, to identify the priority areas for you to concentrate on changing.

4. You'll determine the action steps you're going to take to move towards work you love.

Step 1: define your ideal

Take a new page in your notebook and summarise what you've found out about yourself using each section of the Career Wheel as follows:

- *Values*: what's most important to you in your life and your work?
- *Purpose*: what's the reason you work, what makes work worthwhile for you?
- *Goals*: how does this purpose translate practically for you? Include here the objective you wrote down right at the beginning of your notebook, from chapter 1
- *Talents*: what do you enjoy doing and what are you good at, including your experience, your skills, your knowledge, your attitudes, your natural abilities, your gifts, your interests and hobbies?
- *Control*: what do you need to feel a sense of control over the work you do?
- *Belonging*: what sort of people do you want to work

with and for? What sort of work culture do you feel most at ease in?

- *Recognition*: how do you want to be rewarded? What makes you feel valued and appreciated?
- *Growth*: how do you want to develop, what sort of stimulation do you need, both personally and professionally?

Write down what's key to you using each section in the career wheel to categorise your thoughts. If you'd like to add additional sections to your wheel go right on and do so. This is *your* wheel; customise it so that it works for you.

> There are no right answers; only answers that are right for you

Step 2: identify the matches and the gaps

This is where you compare your ideal with what you have now in your work. Again, write down your thoughts in your notebook.

- *Values*: do your values match what you're doing at the moment in your job? Are any of your values being compromised? Do you find your company's vision and what it's aiming to achieve worthwhile and important? Do you feel motivated to perform well?

- *Purpose*: what's the purpose of the job you do now? Does it relate to the wider purpose of your company? Can you see where it fits in and makes a difference? Do you like that purpose?
- *Goals*: do you have clear goals in your job? Do you know how you're doing, what you're doing well and how you need to improve? Do your goals make sense and motivate you? Do they agree with the first objective in your notebook?
- *Talents*: do you feel confident and competent doing your job? Do you enjoy what you do? Are you being fully utilised? Are there any talents you would like to use more? Less? What talents would you like to develop? Is there sufficient outlet for your creativity?
- *Control*: are you getting the level of control and autonomy you need in your work? Do the demands of your work match what you can give? Are you being asked to do things as part of your job that you struggle with no matter how hard you try? Is there sufficient work/life balance for you? Do your hours match what you'd like? Is the location of your work where you want to be? Do you have freedom to make choices and take responsibility in the way you need? Are you involved and consulted as you'd like?
- *Belonging*: does your company's culture match your

needs? Do you feel a sense of belonging? Do you like your colleagues, your boss? Are your working relationships how you want them? Do you feel that you fit in?

- *Recognition*: do you feel valued and appreciated? Are your opinions sought and listened to as you would like? Is what you're paid appropriate to your role and performance?
- *Growth*: does your current work give you the opportunity to grow? Does it move you closer to the person you want to become? Are you being stretched, challenged and supported as you'd like? Do you feel a sense of excitement and continual learning? Do you see a bright future ahead?

Use your wheel to record every thought that comes into your mind as you go along. Give yourself plenty of time. Remember to note your thoughts about any section you added to customise your wheel too.

Step 3: allocate your satisfaction and importance ratings

This is where you rate each section of your Career Wheel, in terms of how satisfied you are at present in your job, and in terms of how important each section is to you. This will enable you to identify the priority areas for you to concentrate on changing: where the biggest gaps are and what you can do about them to move forward into work you love.

First, give each section of your Career Wheel a rating out of ten in terms of how satisfied you are with it at the moment. A score of ten would mean you're fulfilled and fully satisfied; five would mean there's a significant amount missing; score one and that's an area you are totally unhappy about. Using the diagram, put a cross on the relevant spoke of the wheel for your score in each section. Be scrupulously honest. Include ratings for any sections you added to customise your wheel. Join up the crosses to see what shape your career wheel is in.

Second, give each section an importance rating. A rating of ten would mean this area is critically important for you. It's possible that all sections have equal importance; alternatively it's possible that you will rate different sections with different levels of importance. Using the diagram, put another cross on the relevant spoke of the wheel for your score in each section. Note how the position of this cross compares with the satisfaction rating you've given each section.

Now review your Career Wheel:

- What does it tell you about how satisfied you are with the work you do currently?
- What does it tell you about the priority areas you need to focus on to improve or change?

Step 4: move closer to your perfect work

This is a crucial step: where you start using all the information you've gathered. Tackle each section of your wheel, starting with the areas you've highlighted as the highest priority:

- What's missing? Identify where there is lack. Be precise.
- What needs to be different for your satisfaction scores to increase?
- What needs to change?
- What can you do about it?
- What do you need others to do?
- What support do you need?
- What actions will you take to make these things happen?
- When will you take those actions?

Take your time over this. Think it through. Follow through on the actions you've chosen. Your hard work will be rewarded, I assure you!

Let's take a look at some real life examples. Examples can act as sparks; let's see if any of them contain a spark for *you*.

THINK TWEAK

Ruth was a successful but dissatisfied image consultant.

There was no doubt she was good at her job – her large client list and regular referrals were testament to that – but it was clear that she no longer found her work fulfilling. She had a good income, she chose her own hours, she worked from home, she was using her fashion background in a way that helped other people, making a positive difference to their lives. But the simple matter was that for Ruth what she had wasn't enough. Something was missing. Once she'd allowed herself to accept that fact, we were able to explore *what* was missing.

Her Career Wheel highlighted low scores in *belonging* and *growth* but high scores everywhere else. First, Ruth felt isolated. She missed working in a team; the support, collaboration and camaraderie that teamwork provided. Second, each time she made a positive difference to her clients, each time she saw her clients making great leaps forward, it poignantly reminded her that she had stopped moving forward herself. She wanted some of what she was giving her clients! She needed to find out how she could include what she was missing. Concrete action followed: Ruth investigated how she could collaborate with others of like mind to tweak what she did, so that it helped increase her feelings of belonging and personal growth. She found the answer by becoming part of a supportive and dynamic team that offered a lifestyle management service.

If you know what's missing it's much easier to start looking for it

Maybe what Ruth found also applies to you. Rather than change everything you've got, maybe what's needed is for you to target the specific areas you're not happy with. Perhaps like Ruth there are some key areas missing in your career that you could do something about right now. Study your Career Wheel. What would those be for you? What do you need to do about them?

THINK FIX

I often speak with people who, when they focus on the real problem with their work, find that it comes down to one main issue. A problem in one area can sometimes overspill and profoundly limit enjoyment in everything.

When I worked with James his Career Wheel showed low scores in *talents* and *control*. Probing further, we identified that James hated giving presentations. To add to his misery, he'd had presentation skills training and it hadn't improved the situation for him one bit. In fact, he felt even more of a failure, and was on the brink of deciding he was not suited to his role and needed to change careers. A little investigation and it became clear that his training hadn't sufficiently tackled the area where he struggled most: what he required was personal coaching that gave him specific support where he needed it. Once we'd done this, he was up and off and is now happily engaged in his blossoming management career.

How about you? Like James, does a lack of skills in a particular area hold you back, or does something else get you down – a particular working relationship perhaps, which if you improved would make a vast difference to you? What would it be for you? If there is a specific issue, allow yourself to work as a priority on fixing it, and see the difference it makes.

> Don't let fixable problems distract you

THINK GROW YOUR OWN

Let me tell you the ending to Rachel's story. Rachel, if you remember, told me that she wanted to make a big push forward and achieve an impressive promotion. When we got down to what she really wanted, though, what was important turned out not to be the promotion, but that her talents and skills should be fully utilised. When Rachel reflected on what the promotion would entail, she acknowledged that there was a considerable amount in the new job description that she wouldn't like, and moreover that she would lose a number of the elements of her current job that she enjoyed. If she scored a Career Wheel for her current job and compared it with one for the promotion, what she was now doing was more attractive to her!

> Always play to your abilities

I asked Rachel to write an ideal job description for herself by drawing together the components of what she liked to do and what she did well, taking into account too what she thought would benefit her company. If she imagined she was her own manager and that she'd been set the task of getting the best out of all her staff, what would be her job description? A powerful message emerged: Rachel could be much better utilised by her company if her job was modified to play to her strengths, and, just as important, it would be one that Rachel would delight in. It was breaking with convention, it wasn't the normal promotion route, but what was to stop Rachel putting a case for promotion on her own terms? That is exactly what she did.

What's to stop *you* doing something like that? Imagine yourself as your own manager, set with the task of getting the best out of you. Draw up your ideal job description. Now how about talking to your company about how *that* job would benefit your organisation? Take the initiative – grow your own job.

Maybe it even means your best job is working for *you*. How would that look? Perhaps you've found yourself in a time and place where you want to grow your own job by growing your own company.

THINK LATERALLY

Kate had been an accountant for five years, starting out in one of the Big Four accountancy firms, and, five years on, had progressed in a respectable manner. But she felt like a square peg in a round hole. She didn't really like numbers and hated financial analysis! She liked the people she worked with and there were aspects of her work she enjoyed, but the opportunities to do these were too few and far between.

When we first spoke, Kate didn't know where to turn and felt stuck; as she put it, 'I don't want to lose all the hard work I've put in to get where I am today but if I'm still feeling like this in another five years' time, I'll go mad.'

When Kate completed her wheel, it showed that *talents, growth* and *purpose* needed most attention. Kate felt strongly that she wasn't using her natural talents and skills; she was doing what she *could* do rather than what she *loved* doing. She didn't see any opportunity for growth as she didn't want to be promoted or take on more responsibility in the line of work she was in. Likewise, she didn't feel any sense of purpose in her job.

Together we identified that what she especially enjoyed was managing projects and making sure processes worked effectively; she was terrific at solving problems. She was a natural at explaining complex information to others, through hands-on training, meetings and writing reports. She liked to be involved in things, seeing things through from start to finish and she enjoyed being the linchpin.

When she wasn't imprisoned in financial analysis, Kate also enjoyed being a user representative for her company's financial software system. It wasn't long before Kate had the beginnings of an alternative career role in her sights, working for a financial system provider as an implementation consultant. She would use her knowledge and experience of accountancy but the focus for Kate would be on the skills she loved, and she would be in an environment that gave her the opportunities for growth she craved and a sense of purpose to fire her up once more.

Now let's turn the spotlight on *you*. Think laterally. What sort of businesses are involved with your business? List all the interfaces, and then do some research; find out more about each one. Which are attractive to you? Which would you like to be involved with, to jump across to? What about other departments in your company? What projects have you been involved with that you've enjoyed, or what projects would you like to be involved with? How could you use these to launch a new and rewarding future? What steps could you start taking right now to explore these options further?

> Use where you are as a springboard to jump to where you want to be

THINK EXPERT

Remember Tim? He was a successful salesman, but, like Kate, felt increasingly out of place at work. Tim's waning enthusiasm was also fuelled by his increasing disillusionment with the low level of expertise that new sales people coming into his company had. As he talked, Tim's passion for professional salesmanship shone out. When we linked this passion with his natural talents, a niche role as a high-performance sales trainer and coach emerged. It was a niche he could immediately develop in his current company, while he worked on a longer term goal: to move to a top-flight international sales training organisation that would welcome his language flair and natural showmanship too.

Now you. What happens if you combine your natural talents and call them your expertise? What do you become an expert in? How could you use this to kick-start your perfect career?

> Identify your expertise – it could be your career niche

THINK PORTFOLIO

More and more people are abandoning the practice of doing only one job and instead combining a number of different projects and roles. Are you one of them? What about considering a portfolio career? Maybe this is just what you need to match what you like with what likes you.

> You don't have to stay within a box defined by your company or your job title

Rosie was a TV director. She liked being a TV director. Her Career Wheel scores were high in every area. But there were buts. She also wanted to write. She'd been writing on and off since she was a child and desperately wanted to find time to 'write properly' but her demanding TV schedule didn't allow time for her to pursue writing seriously. The result for Rosie was increasing frustration: even though she enjoyed her TV career, she started to feel trapped.

We started to talk about the possibility of a portfolio career – with TV work as her main 'breadwinner', but with days set aside to write. Although convinced that it would be impossible to persuade her bosses to let her work part time and from home, the prospect of a portfolio career with time for the things she wanted was so enticing that she decided it was worth taking up the challenge. We spent a session together building a powerful case that she could take to her boss. To her delight, she succeeded with her next contract: she's now working from home and doing flexible hours, and has just submitted her first manuscript for a writing competition.

Let's come back to you again. Can you see any parallels in Rosie's story for you? Maybe there's not just one thing you want to do, maybe there are several. If so, how could you work them into a portfolio career? Think about the possibilities. What do you need to do to make those possibilities a reality?

THINK SWITCH

Do you want to switch careers completely? Have you concluded you're in totally the wrong line of work? How does your list of 'want to do's and 'can do's translate into a job? One way to find out could be to wade through a careers reference book until you come across the job descriptions that match your needs. But I prefer a different approach: get very clear about what you want. Keep reminders all around you. These can be in the form of affirmations, pictures, notes – whatever works for you to keep your focus firmly on the direction in which you want to go. Then, rather than squandering your energy lamenting the fact that your current reality doesn't match what you want, start looking for opportunities that will help you move closer to your ideal. Be forever vigilant, from now on, ready to spot the opportunities that *will* present themselves.

It works like this: sit back and take a look around the room you are in. Now make a mental note of everything in the room that is red. Do that now. Close your eyes, then open them again, without looking back into the room. Write down quickly all the red things you saw – and remember, no peeking!

Tell me, how many *blue* things did you see? I would calculate – not many!

> You get what you focus on

When you focus attention on what you want, you may not *immediately* change direction. But keep your new focus and keep alert to every opportunity and it *will* happen. On a jet flying from New York to London, if the pilot makes one degree of error in his entry into the autopilot, the plane will land in Paris. Your one degree of change will make the difference over time too.

Take Chris, a journalist, who at thirty-four decided to retrain as a primary school teacher. He started from the simple awareness that most of his satisfaction came from his free time spent at his local youth club, and in particular from coaching youngsters. He knew he had an ability to relate to children and gain their respect. It led him to investigate opportunities to work with children and to find out that there was a national shortage of male role models in primary schools. He found his fit, pursued it, and is now enjoying a radically different career.

If you're in the wrong place, and the right way forward for you is to make a complete change, what does your Career Wheel tell you about what you need to look for? What will you do about that, starting right now?

THE WORK

1. Create your Career Wheel. What does it tell you about what's important to you in the work you do? How does your current work measure up? What are the priority areas you need to focus on to improve or change? How will you do that?

2. What happens if you *tweak* or *fix*? Is the right

move for you to stay where you are and work on resolving any underlying issues?

3. What happens when you think *laterally*? Look long and hard at all the interfaces around you. How could you use them to build bridges to where you want to go?

4. What happens if you think *grow your own* or *expert*? Are you sitting on a treasure-trove, on talents that you could build into meaningful and enjoyable work for you?

5. What happens if you think *portfolio* or *switch*? You don't need to confine yourself to a box. More and more people are combining different jobs to make one career, or changing careers completely. Are you one of them?

Key idea

When you put together what you like with what likes you, you'll find your perfect match.

5

What's Holding You Back?

Nothing can stop the man with the right mental attitude from achieving his goal; nothing on earth can help the man with the wrong mental attitude

THOMAS JEFFERSON

When Joanne Harris, author of *Chocolat*, was interviewed by *The Times* last year, she remarked: 'I don't have a muse. They must all be busy in London, because you can't get one for love or money here in the North. So, no point sitting waiting for one to come knocking. If I hadn't just cracked on with things, I wouldn't have written even half a book by now.' You, on the other hand, may still be waiting. If you are, then something is holding you back, and our task now is to find out what it is and eradicate it so you can move forward.

Are you waiting for the perfect job to come along, or stalled because what you thought was your perfect job is out of reach? If you're unwilling to move forward until you've found the perfect solution, if – for you – no 'half measures' are allowed, if you've got to get it right, *right now*, then it's just possible that you'll stay stuck where you are for ever.

The truth is, most of us need an amount of trial and error in order to find our way. Most of us don't get the answer, the whole picture, the dream – whatever you choose to call it – in one go. The good news is you don't need the whole solution. For most of us, it's a process. Do you think what you do at twenty you'll still be doing at forty, what you do at forty you'll still be doing at fifty-five? It's unlikely. We change, we grow, we evolve. So does the work we do. What's important is to start taking steps forward. They can be big steps or little steps. The important thing is to get moving.

All through school, a friend of mine just *knew* that he would join the RAF and fly. He just *knew* this would be his perfect job. He even got his glider licence at fifteen and was well on the way to powered flight when he turned up for an eye test and discovered he was red/green colour blind – rather a problem when hurtling along at hundreds of miles an hour and trying to work out whether the plane in front of you is coming towards you or not. In the time it took to blink an eye, his career plan was shattered. My friend then proceeded to meander through jobs in production control until finally he found his niche programming computers, a niche in which he has forged a lucrative and enjoyable career. While all this was happening, he fulfilled his need for speed (and some!) by building cars with jet-sized engines capable of superlative speeds and racing them all over the world. Crucially, although his original dream was blocked, he didn't give up. He found another way through to where he wanted to be, starting from where he was. There's a huge message in this.

> Where you are now is the perfect place to start

Think less in terms of 'there's a perfect job waiting for me somewhere' and think instead of creating stepping stones to bring you closer and closer to what feels perfect for you. Just as you would gradually tone and hone your muscles when you start out on a fitness programme, so you can tone and hone your work to develop your perfect career. Open yourself to the possibility that there are many jobs out there that you can do, and that you'll enjoy doing, right now. Allow yourself to accept that it's not helpful to wait for the perfect match to come to you; believe that you can move towards it.

ARE YOU TERRIFIED OF FAILURE?

Failing and making mistakes are allowed. More than that

– they are essential! Ask successful and happy people the world over about how they got where they are today and they will list failures and mistakes – which they have learned from and built upon to move forward. The man who founded IBM, Thomas J. Watson, said: 'The way to succeed is to double your failure rate.' Abraham Lincoln failed in business aged twenty-two, lost a legislative race at twenty-three, failed again in business at twenty-five, lost the woman he was going to marry when he was twenty-six, had a nervous breakdown at twenty-seven, lost congressional races in his thirties, lost a senatorial race at forty-seven and lost a further senatorial contest at forty-nine. At fifty-two years of age he was elected President of the USA and is now remembered as one of the greatest leaders in world history.

The flip side of allowing yourself to make mistakes and failing is always having to be in control. It's easy to be seduced by this. Unfortunately, there are implications. Being in control feels good, until, that is, you take a wider view and consider what it is you're actually in control of. The simple matter is that always being in control – never doing anything where there's a possibility you may fail, make a mistake, get it wrong – will keep you *small*. Is that really what you want? I don't think so! That's not why you're reading this book, that's not why you're here with me right now. You want bigger, better. So, do your research, do your planning (don't ask for failure!) and then *go get it*. And if you slip and slide a little along the way, it's okay. Steady up your ankles, firm up your laces, take a good look around the terrain and start off again. You can do it.

> Use failure positively. Learn and grow from it. It will move you forward

WHAT WOULD YOU DO IF YOU WEREN'T SCARED?

Fear. It stops the best of us in our tracks at some point. Maybe that's a place you are now. Are you holding back because a little scared voice inside tells you that you have to? Does it whisper words of caution in your ear, warning you that if you move from what you've got it could be even worse? Does it tell you about all the things you could lose? That you shouldn't expect so much? Does it tell you to stick with what you've got, keep your head down, it'll turn out all right in the end?

> Start a new habit to grow your comfort zone continually

Michelle was a musician with an ambition to become a composer, but she was held back by a lack of confidence in her own ability. She'd had a successful career as a pianist before having children, and over the next ten years had retained her love of music but had lost touch with the music scene and felt overcome with nerves at the thought of throwing herself back into it, especially in a field that was new to her. Starting from this point of fear, Michelle did three things. First of all, she acknowledged fully that she *was* scared. Second, she allowed herself to go to the place where she was most scared and faced her biggest fears: together, we explored what it was that made her most anxious. Third, we examined each one of those anxieties objectively. We carefully started to break each fear down into bearable chunks.

For instance, the thought of making speculative phone calls to organisations that might want a composer floored Michelle until she was able to break the task down into smaller things. Making a list of the organisations she'd like to approach; checking if she knew anyone who might know someone (who might know someone) who could arrange an introduction; researching the organisation so that she got a sound feeling for what they were looking for, how she could best help them. *Then* she made the phone call. It was still nerve-racking, she still had to take her courage in both hands, but she also recognised that if she did nothing she'd fail anyway – so the worst she could do would equal doing nothing.

One thing that also helped spur Michelle forward was asking herself this: 'How much would I regret *not* doing something about this; when I'm eighty and looking back on my life, knowing I hadn't tried – how would I feel?' She didn't like the answer she came up with.

By a process of facing and probing her fears and then breaking them down so she could deal with them in smaller chunks, Michelle was able slowly and steadily to grow her comfort zone. Now, three months later, she looks back in amazement at how simple and gentle the whole process has been for her, not without effort but without struggle. And she is writing the music for a stage play at a reputable theatre company in the autumn.

While we're on the subject of fear, let's consider the consequences of success too. Just like the fear of failure, the prospect of success can sometimes be a powerful restraining force. When Ashley spoke to me, a key issue for him was the manuscript for his book. It was nearly complete and he'd had considered feedback that it was good. He even knew an agent who was happy to take him on. However, Ashley hadn't done anything about it. The book was almost written – but languishing. Ashley thought his procrastination was caused by fear of failure, but when we dug deep, what was revealed was a fear of success. His writing contained autobiographical details that he feared would upset his parents. Once he'd uncovered the underlying factor holding him back, he was able to work out a plan of action to talk to his parents and move forward.

WHAT ABOUT MONEY?

Anxiety about financial commitments holds a lot of us back from exploring change. When Colin, a client who started up his own landscape design business, initially thought of 'doing his own thing', he was torn by a deep yearning to leave his job and at the same time a deep fear of the consequences if he did so. He had a mortgage. He ran a car. He had bills to pay. One of the strongest things holding him back was fear of not making enough money to support himself.

Colin is pretty typical of people I work with whose fear of not being able to meet financial obligations keeps them in jobs they don't find satisfying. I know numerous people who stay in well-paid jobs and use their hard-earned cash to compensate for the fact they are so stressed, or frustrated, or bored.

> When you're using money to compensate for your job, consider changing it

If fear of not having sufficient money is holding you back, the first thing I recommend is this: do some sums. How much money do you really need? Audit how you spend your money now and identify what's essential. How could you spend less? Most people, when they do this thoughtfully, find that they can live on considerably less money than they think they can. If money remains an issue, what could you start doing to create more financial freedom for yourself in the future?

If, like Colin, you want to work for yourself but are wary of losing your regular pay cheque, focus on what you'll do to generate income. Rather than wasting energy on worry and disaster scenarios, think about what you can do to make your ideas work in practical financial terms. Put your energy into building success.

This is exactly what Colin did. He took a deep breath and refused to be paralysed by his anxieties; instead he used their energy to galvanise him into action. He thought about how he could get his name known, then took action. He knocked on doors and delivered flyers. He spoke to people he knew – and started to appreciate how word of mouth travels fast for good garden designers. For Colin, it meant getting active: physically getting out and talking with potential clients. He worked through his mental doubts and anxieties by making his body work.

Some of you may have seen the now rather dated film, *Ghostbusters*. I mention it because I think it has a precious message. The soundtrack includes a catchy theme tune with the words, 'Who you gonna call? Ghostbusters!' Whenever you feel scared, I encourage you to get in front of a mirror and sing that song out loud, very loud. Be your own Ghostbuster. If the song doesn't fit for you, find another one – *your* song – one that will rev up your attitude and press your courage button.

WHAT WOULD YOU DO WITHOUT THE STRUGGLE?

How's your stress level? Have you become addicted to stress, always picking the most difficult route, just to prove you can do the hard things? Are you too busy? Too tired? Has struggle become such a habit you can't let go? Have you become so wrapped up in the day-to-day chore of working that you can't see outside it?

Clare worked for a well-known multinational company. Her job was high-powered and involved continuous travel abroad, often to the other side of the world. Although Clare enjoyed travelling and meeting new people, her extreme schedule completely exhausted her, her sickness level was high and her weekends (if she got them) and holidays were spent recuperating. It was only when she had a severe and frightening bout of sickness that she realised she needed to change.

Step back and check that you're not becoming like Clare. Spend some time honestly reflecting on what you're holding on to and how that could be holding you back. Create space and time for yourself to reflect on what you'd do if you didn't feel so stressed, if you weren't so busy or so tired. Now, what will you do about those reflections?

For Clare, it meant accepting that she simply could not sustain the life she was leading. It meant talking to her company doctor and then her boss about her need for more work/life balance. It also meant overcoming her considerable pride that resisted 'copping out' like this. Once she was able to achieve more balance, though, she started to see things differently. She began to recognise how she had created and maintained a vicious circle for herself, how misplaced her pride really was, and how it made complete sense to look for projects that did not exhaust her. Once she opened her mind to this, solutions followed. It's amazing how they do, you know – once you accept what you really need.

> If you're in a vicious 'struggle' circle, it's time to get out

WHAT WOULD YOU DO IF YOU DEFIED CONVENTION?

Although they are breaking down, there are still expectations in our society that can limit our perception of what we can achieve. Think for a moment. Is it possible that you feel constrained by any of these?

Our journalist, Chris, who left journalism to retrain in teaching, had to overcome his apprehension that only 13 per cent of trainee primary teachers were male. Singer Lisa Mafia had to become comfortable as a woman in a man's world – there are thirteen of them in So Solid Crew, and just one of her. Think of Debbie Harry too, the irrepressible lead singer of Blondie. Rather than being crippled by the fear of fading looks and being harshly judged by the celebrity-watching media, she's out there strutting her stuff and the audiences just love it. When Gustave Eiffel erected the Eiffel Tower in Paris in the nineteenth century, he was the first person to use cast iron with no attempt to disguise it; up until then it had only ever been used as hidden framework. Eiffel used it instead in a provocative and defiant way. The majority of his contemporaries condemned the result as ugly and offensive. It's now considered to be one of the masterpieces of world architecture.

Is there something *you* want to do but don't, because concerns about age or gender or popularity get in the way? If so, have courage: throughout history people have succeeded and gained fulfilment in spite of, rather than because of, convention.

> Tell yourself you'll be a convention deviant. See where it takes you

WHAT'S YOUR SUPPORT NETWORK LIKE?

The company we keep is vital. As a coach, I'm acutely aware of how many people live in environments where they lack support and encouragement. I don't think the negative power of criticism can be over-emphasised. We hear regularly of reputable research endorsing the negative impact that being criticised or continually challenged or undermined has on children. The same applies to us as adults. If you don't choose an environment that will best develop you, if you don't have people and things around you helping you, then it's highly likely you will be holding back. Our friends and family don't necessarily mean to constrain us, but inadvertently sometimes they do. Sometimes they want us to stay how we are, not change or move on. Check your support network: is it working for you? If the answer's no, then how can you find the support you need, and when will you do it?

> We all need support. Make sure you have yours

WHAT WOULD YOU DO IF YOU HAD MORE SKILLS?

Are you holding yourself back because you don't think you have enough skills, enough knowledge, enough experience? Let's think about this: what skills, what experience, what knowledge do you need? Let's analyse the gaps. Then let's work out how you can fill them.

> Instead of thinking, 'I can't', ask yourself, 'How could I develop myself so I *can*?'

Scotland's favourite painter is Jack Vettriano. A poster of his most famous painting, *The Singing Butler*, has sold over a million copies and he recently commanded an Old Master price at a record-setting auction, the most ever paid for a painting in Scotland or for any work by a Scottish artist. The son of a coalminer, Vettriano only started painting when he was twenty-one and is completely self-taught. He learned as he went along.

You can too.

ARE YOU THINKING BIG ENOUGH?

Many people hold back because they will not allow themselves to think big. This can be especially prevalent in our British culture, where many of us have been discouraged from 'getting ideas above our station'. Take Graham, one of my clients who hated his job but loved his hobby as a local commentator for an exciting and potential-to-be-Olympic sport. Being a commentator for the Olympics in 2008 was his dream assignment. But it stopped there – *him*, Olympic commentator? No way! When, however, we started to look at who else could do it, no one made it to his list of hopefuls. It was amply apparent that he knew all the key competitors and stakeholders involved in the sport. In short, he was ideally placed to start carving a role for himself if he wanted to do so. What held him back was the thought that his dream was too big. What moved him forward was testing that thought by asking himself, 'If not me, then who else will do it?' Ask yourself if thinking too small could apply to you.

> If you allow yourself to think big, where do you go?

THE WORK

1. Define what it is that's holding you back. How do you sabotage yourself? Put the spotlight on it. Study it. Then work out a plan to deal with it and move beyond it. Be your own Ghostbuster.

2. It doesn't need to be perfect straight away. If the path is challenging and there are excellent views now and again you can be confident that you're moving closer to an inspiring destination.

3. Get the right people around you and think *big*. If your support network lacks support, challenge it to start being on your side or find new friends. Be brave: if you doubled your self-belief, what would you do?

4. Take bite-sized chunks. Tackle scary issues head-on with small tasks and bit by bit this will get the big things done.

5. Concentrate on now and the future, not on the past. If you can't do *Top Gun*, build cars with jet engines in them.

Key idea

Don't get to eighty years old regretting what might have been.

6

Show Yourself Off at Your Best

Tell all the truth but tell it slant

EMILY DICKINSON

No book on doing work you love would be complete without some guidance on how to market yourself effectively if you decide to apply for a new role – so it's time to get very practical again, and talk about your CV and the way you present yourself in interviews. Alternatively, if you've decided that doing your own thing is more you, we'll have some time here dedicated to getting that project going, too. Let's go!

I must admit that most people, when they come to talk to me about the subject of their CV and how they can interview better, usually fall into one of two categories. Either their eyes are glazing over and a yawn is already tugging at the corner of their mouths at the prospect of the work we have ahead of us, or they have that rabbit caught in the headlights look that says, 'Help me now, *please*!' If you fit in either of these categories, or even a completely different one, don't worry: I'm here to help and get you moving forward. I'm going to share with you the most important tips that have helped my clients over the years. By the time we've finished working together, I'd like you, like them, to have a big smile on your face and be ready to step out positive and enthusiastic, knowing you can show yourself off at your best. Big ambition? Of course! Why not? You can do it.

YOUR CV

Think about the last few films you went to see at the cinema. The likelihood is that the reason you went to at least one of them is that you saw the trailer, found what you saw appealing, and made a mental note to see that film. Now imagine you're stuck waiting for a train and you decide to kill some time in the local bookshop. Before you decide to buy a book, what would you do? Most of us would read the back cover and get a feel for whether this is our type of book or not.

If we look at what makes a good trailer or a good book cover they have three important elements in common. First, they highlight the best bits. Second, they put the best bits together in a way that connects with us. And third, they visually stimulate us in a way that entices us to want to read or see more. This is how I'd like you to start thinking about your CV: as your trailer if you were a film, or your cover if you were a book.

Showcase your best bits

Whoever reads your CV does *not* want to read a dull narrative of duties and responsibilities you've had – if they did, they might as well ask you to send them your job descriptions. They do want to know what you've done, but more than that they want you to tell them what you've *made* of the jobs you've had. They want to know about your achievements, what people will remember you for, what you'll be missed for when you've gone. These are your best bits.

Anyone can write, for example: *Responsible for project managing and providing technical expertise to implement the corporate help desk system,* but what does it actually mean? What did you truly do? In this case, the person I was coaching single-handedly drove the implementation of the system, he was the company expert, he overcame considerable staff apathy and resistance in the process and he delivered on time and within budget.

So what we wrote was this: *Successfully and single-handedly implemented the corporate help desk system, over-*

coming considerable staff apathy and resistance, achieving live status smoothly on time and within budget.

Can you see the difference? Rather than writing what his job description said, he wrote what he actually did.

Wherever practical, give quantifiable evidence of your achievements. If you improved something, show how you've measured that – how you know you did it. For instance, let's say you know you 'increased customer satisfaction'; well, how do you know that? Are there satisfaction surveys you can quote, or customer compliments, or complaint statistics?

The other thing your reader wants is punchy, first-person 'doing' words, rather than dry and distant third-person ones, at the beginning of each point they read. For instance, rather than say 'responsible for managing', simply say 'managed' and take care not to repeat yourself, especially the first word at the beginning of each point – or it will read like your seven times table! So, sprinkle in words like 'initiated', 'developed', 'negotiated', 'organised', 'improved' where they are pertinent.

> Present yourself at your best, back it up with proof, and do it in a succinct and active way

Connect with your reader

Think again about those film trailers you've seen and book covers you've read. Some appealed to you, others didn't. Those that appealed to you connected with you in some way, didn't they? That's what we need to do with your CV: make it connect with the person and organisation you send it to.

The best way to do this is to get yourself as familiar as possible with the sort of person who will be reading your CV and the sort of company you will be sending it to. The research you do at this stage will pay dividends. As a minimum, check to see if there is a website and if so read it, inspect any marketing material produced, any press coverage, and talk to people to find out if anyone knows any useful snippets of information about the company you're targeting. If there's a job advert, don't forget that either. All these things contain helpful information that you can use to home in on what the employer is truly looking for. Study all the information you have and write a checklist for yourself that describes the sort of person they need. Refer to this checklist constantly while tailoring your CV and accompanying letter.

I'll always remember going to the interview for my first 'proper' job, a graduate trainee scheme with the NHS. Throughout the interview, I was struck by the number of times the word 'accountable' was used by the panel. At my next interview, with a different panel this time, I was asked what I thought the most important issue facing the NHS was at that time. 'Accountability,' I said! And proceeded to expand on why, because I'd done some homework in the meantime. To be honest, it was more by chance than planning that I managed to tune in like this, and had I done my homework before that first interview I'd have tuned in then; there was certainly the information around to help me to do so.

You can be better than I was then – do your homework before you complete your CV, and make sure that every CV you send out is tailored to catch each individual employer's attention. An ability to tune in to the employer's situation, where they are at, is crucial. Get focused on what will interest *them*.

Let me give you an example. Jackie was a trainer who wanted to work as an associate for a sought-after training consultancy. When we constructed her CV, we ensured it contained all her best bits, and we also tailored it for bespoke appeal. The consultancy listed profiles of its other trainers. From studying these closely, Jackie was able to determine where her skills and experience could potentially complement and expand the service currently provided. She then filtered her best bits to this effect. As a result, rather than simply sending a CV that said, 'Hi, here I am; take a look at me!' she sent a CV that said, 'Hi, I think I can help you!' and then demonstrated in her CV how.

Think selective and high-class marketing, not mass-market mail shot

Focus on great presentation

Just as you like films and book covers that stimulate you visually, employers like CVs that are presented well.

Key to this is structure, and one that works is this: at the very top have your name (big and bold) and contact details, followed by a short profile of yourself: a synopsis in a few lines of what they'll be getting if they employ you. This synopsis shows you at your best; it's succinct and positive, and it's geared towards what you know they need. Let me demonstrate with a couple of examples.

How about this one, a candidate aiming at in-house promotion to project manager. Although having no formal project management skills she is keen and focused: *A motivated and resourceful self-starter, with first-rate organisation and relationship-building skills. A creative problem-solver who is able to identify business needs effectively through highly developed analytical and interpretive skills. Commercially aware, pragmatic and flexible with the drive and personality to make things happen.*

Or this one, an engineer looking to take on part-time lecturing at a local college: *A professional mechanical engineer with over thirty years' industry experience and a track record of technical and managerial excellence in engineering design and development. A first-class man manager and motivator, with the ability to develop and train others from diverse academic and cultural backgrounds. Experienced in working with all methodologies from formal classroom-style training to informal one-to-one coaching and mentoring. Strong team player and problem-solver with a practical, enthusiastic approach. HNC Mechanical Engineering.*

After your profile I suggest you include a bullet point section to summarise the key, relevant skills, experience and achievements you have, and follow this by a succinct summary of your employment history, in reverse chronological order. At the end you can then detail any qualifications and finally, if you would like to, some insight into your interests and hobbies.

Let's not forget the basics. Spelling and grammar: do make sure you've got these right. Avoid fancy fonts and overcrowding: some white space will make your CV easier on the eye. Use quality stationery and don't fold it if you're sending by post; if you're e-mailing check that there isn't an unwanted white page at the end before you click 'send'.

> Keep it neat, simple and classy

There are two words I want you to burn into your mind as interview priorities: 'warm' and 'engaged', because even the best candidates can fail at interviews if they don't show these qualities. Just as we feel connected when we watch a film trailer we like, being warm and engaged is the way we make our interviewer like and feel connected with us. Always remember that you're being employed as a *person*, not simply a list of tasks to be achieved, and that you will need to get along with other people, to fit in smoothly and make a positive difference to the team you work within.

Follow the four-point plan

As you prepare for your interview, focus on this four-point plan:

1. **What does the job need you to do?** Thoroughly appraise all the information you have. Now summarise in writing what the priorities are in this job.

2. **Exactly what does the company do?** What impact will this have on you, doing this job? What are the significance and consequences for you as job holder? Do your research so that you understand the wider

context of your role and the issues faced. Add these thoughts to your summary.

3. **What sort of person are they looking for?** If you were in their shoes, if you were the other side of the desk on interview day, what would you be looking for? What experience, skills, knowledge and personal qualities do you need to demonstrate to prove that you can do this job how they want it to be done? Add it to what you've written.

4. **How will you do that?** Think about the experience, skills, knowledge and personal qualities you have and how these are now relevant. What examples can you provide of real-life situations you've dealt with effectively? How will you bring out your strengths? Write it down.

Now take everything you've written and put it into your own words. This will ensure that you're not simply quoting the job spec and it will get you thinking in terms of pertinent and pithy interview answers. Make your words active and use the first person. Write how you'd talk.

For example, if the company focuses on building effective business relationships and views this as a way to differentiate itself from its competition, then you may have something like this on your sheet:

1. One of my top priorities in this job is building effective business relationships.

2. They need me to be committed to the importance of quality client relationships and how these can differentiate us from the competition. ('To do' list: identify competition and research its strengths and weaknesses.)

3. They'll want someone who can: build rapport and gain credibility with clients quickly; who has personal impact; who can converse easily with senior people; who knows what they are talking about; who can deal practically and effectively with high-level issues; proactively manage problems; make sure we deliver what we say we deliver.

4. I'm totally committed to the importance of building quality client relationships; I've seen what can happen to business when client relationships aren't managed well. I also understand a quality relationship doesn't mean simply running around trying to keep the customer happy. (Example about expectation management that shows me off in a positive light.) I've got a sound grasp of the key skills that are needed to build relationships. For instance, I can build rapport and gain credibility with clients quickly because I make sure I do my homework and know what I'm talking about. I'm at ease with senior people, I deal practically with

issues – I'm the sort of person who doesn't wait for problems to happen. I make sure I'm keeping a close eye on accounts so I'm aware of any issues. (An example that's relevant to show me off being effective in this way.)

Do you get the idea? Interview preparation in this way will raise the quality of your answers and your confidence at the same time.

Master the tricky questions

What about tricky questions that might come up in the interview? Let's cover three classics.

To start with: *What are your weaknesses*? There are two rules here. First, wherever possible select weaknesses that will *not* have a serious impact on the interviewer's perception of your ability to do the job. At its simplest, an inability to get in to work bang on 9 a.m. for instance, will not have a big influence if the job is flexitime. Second, be truthful but always give anything you say a positive, benefit-to-them twist. For instance, one of my clients had an interview for a surgeon's post lined up, and she wholeheartedly wanted the job. But she had also applied for, and been awarded, a research fellowship in another speciality and she was concerned that this would be construed as a weakness in the interview: highlighting a lack of commitment on her part. When we explored further, though, the positive, benefit-to-them twist emerged: she had already achieved the relevant research fellowship that was directly applicable to the interview post, so in order to continue learning she needed to seek alternative fellowships, to keep herself aware and knowledgeable and tuned in to continual self-development. Thus, from a perceived weakness, a strength emerged. Even if you have a weakness that you find very difficult to see anything positive in, demonstrate that you are doing something about it. Show that you're not complacent. Bear in mind too that you don't know about the other candidates – you may have strengths where they have weaknesses.

Second: *Where do you see yourself in five year's time*? If you don't know, there's no need to get in a tangle with this one. Instead make it clear that your approach is to keep focused on doing a good job and being alert to change and that in order to do that, you're keen to keep expanding your skills and taking on new assignments. Make it clear that you're very aware that what companies need is someone who can respond positively to and be ready to take on new challenges which often can't be predicted – and that's the sort of person you are.

Third: *What salary are you looking for*? I suggest you look at this from three angles. 1. What's the market rate for this job? Be clear about the market and your worth within it. 2. Is there any reason for you to believe your company could pay more or less than this rate? Market rates by definition are averages; some employers pay less, some pay more. 3. What's your personal rate – what do you want to earn? What's your ideal, and what's your minimum? How does this fit with the other two? Using all three answers, where will you now position yourself? Be realistic. Don't oversell, but don't undersell yourself either. And always remember that once you start the job the salary you've agreed will form the basis for all further reviews.

Roll your sleeves up

Let's talk some more about being warm and engaged. Good news: you've already started, by preparing for your interview using *real* language, not stilted management-consultant-speak. Get into this mode more by thinking of the interview as your first day on the job. Metaphorically speaking, roll your sleeves up. So, what would you want to know about this job in order to get moving on the priorities? Immediately you do this you'll start to hear the sorts of questions you need to ask in the interview. When it comes to the questions they ask you in the interview, take each question as though you were talking with your new colleagues as the incumbent already. Think about that – you'd want to impress them and make them like you at the same time, wouldn't you? That's exactly the result you're aiming for in the interview. I can see you leaning forward a little, listening intently, being thoughtful about what you would do, energetic, enthusiastic, asking questions to check your understanding and so you know you've got to grips with what's needed. Take the pressure off yourself to be a *performer* and make yourself into a *doer* instead. Just try it and see the difference it can make.

DOING YOUR OWN THING

If you decide to set up on your own, then everything you've read so far is relevant and I urge you to apply it just the same. For 'CV', read 'marketing material' and for 'interview' read 'talking with potential clients'. Ensure your marketing material highlights your best bits, and is put together in a way that will attract and benefit your target client. Use quality stationery and make sure it has visual appeal. And don't forget to take advantage of the help that exists for people setting up their own business – contact Business Link, for instance, and your bank's small business adviser.

Follow the four-point plan:

1. **What do your clients want?** Do your research and then thoroughly appraise all the information your research has told you.
2. **Think about the wider context.** This means anything

that could impact, positively or negatively, on your ability to attract people as clients. Know what your competitors are doing; understand and tune in to the factors that influence your clients' willingness to purchase.

3. Put yourself in your clients' shoes. What experience, skills, knowledge and personal qualities do you need to demonstrate to prove that you can offer what they need?

4. How will you do that? What examples and case studies can you give them, to bring what you offer alive, to connect with them, to demonstrate you understand their situation and can deal appropriately and confidently with it? How will you answer their tricky questions? And finally, how will you be warm and engaged and say, 'Hey, hello, I'm here to help, and here's how!'

THE WORK

1. Gather all the information you need for your CV. Details of your past jobs, things you know you do well, things you enjoy doing, your personal strengths and talents, details of the post you're applying for. If you're sending a speculative application, create your own spec of the sort of job you're aiming to get and work from that starting point.

2. **Pick out your best bits.** Then present them in a bullet-point, punchy and active format that highlights any supporting evidence and that is relevant to whoever is going to read it.

3. **Write a short and succinct personal profile about yourself.** Make sure it describes you at your best. On a good day. And again, ensure it's relevant.

4. **Prepare thoroughly for interview.** Follow the four-point plan. Be prepared for difficult questions.

5. **Make sure you're ready to be warm and engaged.** Be positive and enthusiastic. Roll your sleeves up. Put yourself in their shoes. Talk real language. *Their* language.

Key idea

Warm and engaged people land the best jobs.

7

Keep It Perfect

Our aspirations are our possibilities

SAMUEL JOHNSON

One of the most rewarding things about being a personal coach is that I get to help each individual I work with make the most of what they've got. In this last chapter, I'm going to share with you the key tips that my own experience and that of my clients has taught me – to ensure that I help *you* make the most of what *you've* got.

1. EVERY DAY IN EVERY WAY, GET BETTER

'Every day in every way I'm getting better.' Although I know this is an overused cliché, working with my clients has given me solid evidence that if you *work* this cliché, the results will be compelling. First, people who successfully keep their work perfect for them use and continue to develop their strengths. Second, they deal with their weaknesses.

Grow your strengths. Once you've learned what they are, find ways to use them continually, and find outlets to use them in new ways, too. Actively seek out assignments to push your boundaries a little further, take courses to consolidate and deepen your knowledge, and become a mentor to others to share and expand the skills you have. Keep sharp about the strengths you display when you're at your best and develop them to your advantage by using them in all areas of your life. Reject any form of complacency.

Deal with your weaknesses. Remedy those you can, and compensate for those you can't. Can you recall when you learned to drive? All the different things you had to remember to do, to co-ordinate – did you, like me, end your first lesson thinking you'd never get the hang of it? Do you now often find yourself driving from A to B and not even recalling doing it, the actions have become so easy and automatic? It can be the same with our weaknesses. Sometimes what we call our weaknesses stay weaknesses because we don't push ourselves beyond the first lesson.

When I coached John in setting up his business, one of the things he dreaded was the 'marketing bit'. He hated the idea of having to do what everyone recommended he do – *network*: the very thought of it gave him palpitations. He was not a natural talker; he wasn't at ease in large social gatherings; on top of that he found the whole concept of networking (or brown-nosing as he preferred to call it) distasteful. After a lively and firm conversation about what networking is about (I prefer the Australian translation: dropping in on your buddies to share a beer), we tackled the real issue. Unfamiliar territory is always a little alarming at first. It's often easier to listen to our subconscious shouting at us to get back on familiar ground than persevere on new territory. John got there – in the end! So can you. Once you've recognised your weaknesses, work on them and overcome them. Keep moving forward.

In practical terms, at your next performance review for your job make sure you know what you need to do in order to achieve the next level of rating. Ask your boss to be specific. For example, ask: 'What exactly do I need to be doing differently in order to get to the next performance level, and how will you measure me?' Make it clear that you want to have detailed advice. Don't accept a woolly answer. Your goal is to leave the room with a full understanding of what it is you need to do, how you need to change, and how you will be measured. Aim to be the best. And if your company doesn't do reviews, have the conversation with your boss anyway.

Invest in yourself. Gone are the days (if they ever existed) when you could expect your company to take responsibility for your development. You are responsible for yourself and your career: your success and your future are in your own hands. Source training courses and workshops that will develop you or fill gaps in your skills and knowledge. If your employer is not able or willing to fund you, pay for yourself. As well as taking control of your own development, you'll make sure you attend events that you really do need.

Or go bespoke, fast-track yourself and get a coach. Together with skilled performance coaching, you'll have a creative sounding board for your ideas and an objective viewpoint, uncompromised by any in-house politics. Build your confidence, overcome obstacles, develop your working relationships. Focus on exactly what you need to focus on; tackle exactly what you need to tackle.

> Take responsibility for your own development. Keep growing who you are in the best way that you can

2. TEAM UP AND SHARE

When I changed career direction from HR to Customer Services I joined a software company and found myself suddenly thrown into a situation where I knew nothing. My job was to be help desk support for HR software products, but as I rapidly learned, my HR knowledge was not one iota of use unless I had software skills, which I did not. I had never even turned on a PC before. I graphically remember my first day. I was sat in front of a computer and told to 'use the tutorial' to teach myself the system. Cautiously I leaned forward and switched on the button on the screen in front of me. I waited . . . nothing happened. I looked around me. Everyone was so busy; phones were ringing; there was an air of much to do and not enough time to do it. I looked back at my screen and pressed the button again. Suddenly a gentle Welsh voice said into my ear, 'You've not used a computer before, have you, my love?' and a lovely tall Welshman proceeded to show me the box under the desk where I later learned the computer kept its brains.

At that moment I had to make a decision. There I was, fresh from a successful career in HR and eager to get in and make my new mark, suddenly immobilised by an acute awareness that I knew less than the sixteen-year-old youth trainee. I could shrivel up with shame and embarrassment or I could accept my ignorance and vulnerability and ask for help. I chose to ask for help.

Seek out and surround yourself with others who will mentor you, challenge you, support you. Continually ask yourself, 'What support do I need to ensure I succeed?' Guard against misplaced pride that doesn't want you to ask for help. Help yourself though – make sure you don't become a burden to your colleagues. I lost count of the number of notebooks I kept over the years in that job, recording every bit of information I was told until slowly and painfully even I, one of the most IT-illiterate people I know, started to see some logic to how those software products functioned.

Just as important, be a coach and mentor to others. Share what you know, your skills, the short cuts you've learned. Don't let someone learn the hard way just because you had to. If that's not the culture in your organisation, then make it the culture. Pioneer it!

I went on to manage that customer services department and we developed what I believe to be one of the strongest knowledge-sharing cultures around. I will always remember a colleague from another department walking in one day and observing, 'You know, there's a whole different feeling when you walk into this bit of the building – everyone seems to work so well together and genuinely want to help each other. It's like a little oasis. It recharges my batteries just being here.'

Wouldn't you like to work in a place like that? Then make sure you do your bit to make it possible.

> Be an enhancer, and seek out others who enhance. Look for ways to share your knowledge and skills

3. BE YOUR OWN CHAMPION

The relationships we foster at work are crucial. Think beyond your immediate sphere of influence. You may be liked and respected by your boss and your team, but is that enough? Who else is aware of your existence and what you can do? No matter how supportive your boss and team are, they might not like to spread the word about you too positively in case someone else sees you and wants you. It's human nature – we don't like to let go of a good thing, no matter how unconsciously we do it. So get your light out from under that bushel. How can you raise your profile and be more visible, communicating what you do and what you are capable of doing to significant others in the company? Here are four suggestions for starters.

First, be a mover and a shaker. Look for ways in which you can make a difference. Consider volunteering to represent your area in a company initiative (and take a positive, active role), or giving a presentation on your team's work and how it contributes to the company (and ask for suggestions on how it could contribute more). Add to the success of your company. How can you help it to make money, save costs, make procedures smoother, raise customer satisfaction, make your team stronger? How can you share your ideas and your knowledge? Get involved. Be energetic.

Second, develop a wide network of contacts. Make

sure you take every opportunity to get to know people and what they do. Think about how they could help you and, just as important, how you can help them. Have a mind to this fact too: more and more vacancies are being filled by people who know people. Employers don't always advertise vacancies, so the wider your network of contacts, the more opportunities you'll get to hear about; and one of those opportunities could be just the perfect next move for you.

> Your career will be influenced by your relationships with others just as much as your competence on the job

Third, get a mentor. Approach someone more senior in your organisation, not in your direct management tier, who you respect. Ask them if they will mentor you.

Lastly, see yourself how others see you. It's easy to forget when we go about our daily work that everything we do speaks volumes about us. Just for a minute, imagine that a secret camera is following you around, watching your every move and listening in to your conversations. Imagine too that the footage is going to end up on the MD's desk. When it does, would what they see and hear make you cringe in the slightest? If so, what do you need to do, or stop doing, right now? Make a new commitment: 'I'm great on camera!'

4. KEEP ALERT AND NIMBLE

Another thing about my most successful clients is this: they're not afraid to change direction. Even if they've found the star that they want to hitch their wagon to, they are prepared to change stars if it feels right. As we grow and evolve, as different people come into our lives, our needs can change. Making sure we keep tuned in and aware of that is vital. A great way to do this is to schedule yourself time for regular career health checks to review your Career Wheel and make sure you're still heading in a direction you find energising and inspiring.

In 2003, following a life-threatening illness and six months of painful and difficult recovery, the singer and guitarist Chris Rea decided to found his own record label, Jazzee Blue. During his illness, he'd realised that he had become distanced from his reason for being an artist in the first place and so he made a commitment to perform the sort of music he really wanted to perform, rather than follow the commercial mainstream. His sold-out Blue Jukebox tour in 2004 was testament to the fact he had still managed to make a sound commercial decision; more importantly, for him, his music was once again 'a main part of my life and soul'.

It doesn't have to be a life-threatening illness that warns you your career is going off course. Watch where you're going and you'll be able to steer your rudder to keep on your perfect path.

> Schedule regular career MOTs with yourself to keep your career on track

Use this simple tool to help you. It's called stop – start – continue.

- What do you need to *stop* doing in order for your work to be better?
- What do you need to *start* doing?
- What are you doing that's absolutely spot on – what do you need to make sure you *continue* doing?

Then make sure you do all those things.

5. IF THINGS GO WRONG, ACT

If you expect that everything will always go the way you want it to, you're probably going to be disappointed. Let's use an analogy. If you're a sporting person, imagine your favourite team is playing against its arch-opponent and you're watching from the stands. Now let's zoom in a little closer.

Your team has been playing its heart out in the first

half and you are jubilant when they score the first goal. Boy, they deserved it; it's been a really tight contest but their superior skill won through. The stands go wild. The next fifteen minutes are a bit slow though, the pace goes down and you are starting to get a bit frustrated at the lack of action . . . when suddenly out of nowhere one of the opponent's players darts through and scores. Oh no! Where did that come from? Your former jubilation quickly turns to horror. The pace picks up again and your team rises to the challenge. They're definitely taking charge. They're making a run . . . will they . . . The whistle blows for half time. You're left with a feeling of anticipation and you can't wait for the game to restart.

If things always go our way, we can get lazy, complacent. If things are too easy for us, we lose our edge. We can start to feel frustrated and bored and flat. If things always go our way our attention can wander, we lose our focus; moreover our attention can shift to less constructive matters. If something goes wrong, on the other hand, we need to regroup, upgrade our thinking and what we do with that thinking. We re-engage. We ramp up our game.

It's the same with your work. If things don't go as you want them to, regroup. Consider your options. If you go for an interview and don't get the job, rather than bemoaning your misfortune, get analysing. What went wrong? What could you do better? What do you need to do about that? How will you use the experience to ramp up your game?

Take the advice of the ancient mystic, Rumi: take sips of the pure wine being poured, not minding that you've been given a dirty cup. Contemplate too: sometimes when things don't go our way there's a good reason they don't.

> Sometimes we get what we need not what we want

Take the highs with the lows – because it's the lows that make the game. After all, watching the match highlights that night was great, but if you weren't at the game you missed so much, didn't you?

6. DON'T LOSE SIGHT OF WHAT YOU ALREADY HAVE

There's an experiment going on at the moment, led by Dr Martin Seligman, American psychologist and critically acclaimed author of the book, *Authentic Happiness*. By collating research from volunteers across all continents, Seligman's mission is to discover how to increase the human potential for happiness. One of the greatest insights that's resulted to date is scientific confirmation that it does us good to keep escalating our goals, to keep seeking to improve our lot in life, so long as we don't become so fixated with what we want to achieve that we lose sight of what we already have.

It's tempting when we're striving to get better all the time to forget to value what we've already achieved, how far we've come. A common factor among my most successful clients is that they are adept at recalling the achievements they had, in the past, and keeping them meaningful. Another factor they have in common is this: acknowledging when other people have helped them attain those achievements, and saying thank you to them for it.

> Maintain a list of your achievements, your proudest moments, and remember to say thank you to the people who helped

7. YOU HAVE A CHOICE

Ultimately, finding work you love and continuing to love it comes down to your own choice. You can manage your career or you can let it manage you. You can create opportunities or wait for them to come to you. For so many people, the overriding obstacle to moving forward and finding work they love is making the commitment to do it. So, I ask you to do this:

commit to moving forward and do something to demonstrate that commitment. Then do something else. You get the idea! Why not start right now?

THE WORK

1. Grow your strengths, work on your weaknesses. Every day, in every way, ensure you're getting better. Actively seek out ways to grow your comfort zone.

2. Be your own champion. Get your light out from under its bushel. Identity the major stakeholders in your company and find ways to make an impact in a positive way. Be involved and energetic.

3. Count your blessings. Value what you have as well as what you want to achieve. Take time out to reflect on how far you've come and appreciate what you've gained. Make sure you say thank you to the people who've helped you.

4. Use failure as feedback. Use setbacks to tone and hone and remember that watching the game would be so boring if all you saw were the goals.

5. Drive with due care and attention and schedule regular MOTs. Only you can manage your career. I urge you to do so. Set aside regular slots to review where you are and where you want to be and play the stop – start – continue game to make sure you keep on target.

Key idea

Wherever you are now, it's the right time and place to start. Doing nothing is no longer an option. Whatever you do today will make a difference.

And finally: you've been terrific. You *are* terrific. I wish I could be with you now: cheerleading and championing you. Just see the potential you have – and step by step, bring it out. You can make it happen. I know you can. Go on – go strut your stuff!